59 THINGS
YOU SHOULD KNOW ABOUT
YOUR CAT

Published by Sourcebooks
P.O. Box 4410, Naperville, Illinois 60567-4410
(630) 961-3900
sourcebooks.com

Originally published in 2022 in the United Kingdom by LOM ART, an imprint of Michael O'Mara Books Limited.

Cataloging-in-Publication Data is on file with the Library of Congress.

Printed and bound in China.
OGP 10 9 8 7 6 5 4 3 2 1

59 THINGS
YOU SHOULD KNOW ABOUT
YOUR CAT

WRITTEN BY
ALISON DAVIES

ILLUSTRATED BY
NAMASRI NIUMIM

sourcebooks

Introduction

If you are the owner of a much-loved feline, you'll know how much joy they bring. From delighting you with their antics, to snuggling up when the going gets tough, your BFF (best furry friend) knows a kitty cuddle is the purrfect cure-all. What's more, it's delivered in style, because cats have class. They're curious, cute, and seriously quirky; a conundrum wrapped in fur. One minute they're lapping up attention on your laptop; the next they're off chasing something that you can't see or hear, but they know is there. You can spend a lifetime trying to work out what makes your cat tick, and you'll only scratch beneath the collar, but while each pussycat is a puzzle, there are some essential facts that every cat lover should know to gain a little much-needed insight.

They may spend most of their day in the land of nod,

but there's a lot going on behind the scenes. From using different body parts to show how much they care, to mimicking your chatter, clever cats have it figured out when it comes to getting what they want. After all, they've been doing it for thousands of years, and they're no strangers to the hard sell. Able to see a gap, and fit snugly into it, the cat is a maestro at most things. What it can't do with paws and claws, it masters with kitty cuteness. Feisty, flighty, and feline fabulous, your cat can certainly teach you a thing or two when it comes to poise and balance, and as for self-care, the discerning kitty knows that a tip-top beauty regime will make it feel like the cat that got the cream—so what if it takes most of the day?

Your moggy is a marvel, and it likes to share the love with you. From the power of the purr, to the scent glands in its fur, you're a part of Team Kitty, which is why it's good to study up on all things cat. There will always be something new to discover with these mysterious creatures, and I hope this book will bring you a little closer to understanding these feline beauties.

Cats are right or left pawed

Whether they're swiping roast chicken from your dinner plate, or chasing butterflies, they'll favor one paw the most. Male cats tend to be lefties, while for the female of the species, it's right all the way!

Cats love to sunbathe

Clever kitties know the sun will keep them warm while they're in the land of nod because their body temperature drops. They even alter position to catch the best rays! Like humans, they can burn, but a dab of sunscreen on the nose and tips of the ears keeps these bathing beauties safe.

Cats don't have a sweet tooth

Cats don't care which way the cookie crumbles. The truth is, they can't taste the sweet stuff. With only a few hundred taste buds, they're not the gourmets we think they are. They might be feline fussy at mealtimes, but they're just keeping you on your toes.

Cats have a great beauty regime

Fancy felines preen and pamper between thirty and fifty percent of the time, which might sound like a lot to us. Far from being vain, the polished pussycat practices self-care. Grooming helps to promote blood flow, cools the coat, and also masks your cat's scent from predators, while the natural oils that are distributed keep the fur *fabulous, darling*!

Cats know how to strut their stuff

Sharing the graceful saunter of the much leggier giraffe and camel, cats step out with both right feet and then left, in a delicate dance that moves half the body at once. It's no wonder they always steal the show.

Cats dream just like us

It's not unusual for your cat to slip into a dream during a quick nap, with an REM sleep cycle every twenty-five minutes. Whether they're sweet dreams of gentle tummy tickles or mountains of smoked salmon succulence, you can bet your feline has fun. On the flip side, they get nightmares too, but nothing that a cuddle from their human can't chase away.

Cats ignore you on purpose

Felines live by their wits and whims. It doesn't matter that you've spent hours scouring the streets, cat treats in hand, while your moggy gives you the slip. It can hear you, recognize your voice, and even understand its name, but if it's not in the mood, it won't play the game.

Cats are contortionists

All felines can squeeze into the teeniest, tiniest spaces thanks to their free-floating collarbones, which connect forelimbs to shoulders and give them ninja-like flexibility. A supple rotating spine provides even more elasticity, along with cushioned discs between each vertebra. To you, it's a chink of light beneath the washing machine; to your cat, it's a home away from home!

Cats don't have eyelashes

They might have a few stray hairs around the eyes, but rather than eyelashes, cats have an extra eyelid called a haw to protect their eyes, sometimes seen when they blink or are asleep. Whitish in color, this membrane is not the prettiest sight, but it protects the cornea from infection and keeps your cat's peepers primed!

Cats have kindles

A group of adult cats is known as a clowder, while a group of kittens is known as a kindle. Although a litter has the same mom, it is possible for each kitten to have a different dad, which explains why some siblings are so unalike.

Cats' tongues are lethal

Their tongues feel like sandpaper because they're covered in tiny spines that act like hooks, which tear the meat from the bones of its prey. Shaped like miniature cat's claws, these spikes, called papillae, are made of keratin. Mouthful of fingernails, anyone?

Cats' ears are finely tuned instruments

Each ear is a muscular powerhouse, with thirty-two muscles that rotate and swivel at 180 degrees. Compared to the outer ear of a human, which has only six muscles, it's no surprise your pussycat can hear the rustle of cat treats from several streets away!

Cats are super speedy

Most felines can move quickly, especially when the fridge door is open. Your pussycat is no exception and, with a little motivation, has the ability to reach 30 mph without breaking a sweat.

Cats love a cardboard box

Forget the latest play toy—the box it came in is far more interesting. It's made from cozy cardboard, which is naturally insulating, and covered on most sides, making it the hideout of choice. Your kitty feels safe, secure, and ready to pounce on human and feline intruders.

Cats use their heads

When your cat bops you with its head, it's not to knock you out. It's the feline way of saying, "Hi, how are you doing?" From getting your attention to creating a colony scent, which other cats can pick up, your fur buddy is making a statement: "I'm yours and you're mine. End of story."

Cats *need* to scratch

Yes, really! It's essential moggy maintenance, helping to remove the pesky outer layer of your pussycat's claws, though it's also used to get your attention. Cats do it to scent-mark territory like their favorite armchairs and express their excitement too. The next time your cat digs in a claw when you walk through the door, be glad – they're just hyped that you're home!

Ginger cats have freckles

These tiny brown and black speckles are the result of a genetic condition called lentigo, which means they have more pigment-producing cells. These multiply, causing a flurry of dark spots around the mouth and on their paw pads. #CatCuteness

Cats' noses know EVERYTHING

It may be as cute as a button, but a cat's nose hides more than 200 million sensors and can sniff out trouble in a heartbeat. Whether on the hunt for a catnip mouse or finding its way home after a night on the town, the nose has it.

Cats like it when you're smelly

Stinky shoes and sweaty socks might not seem appealing to you, but to your cat they're feline heaven. Every scent has a secret: a message that reveals where you've been and who you've been with – and because you belong to the same social group, they'll want to get up close and personal with your scent and add their own to the mix.

Cats' brains are ninety percent similar to yours

It might be much smaller at around 2 inches (5 cm) in length and a different shape, but a cat's brain shares the same structure as a human one. One key difference is the cerebellum, which is much bigger in cats and all about balance and coordination. What your kitty lacks in common sense it makes up for in moves and grooves.

Cats can jump six times their body length

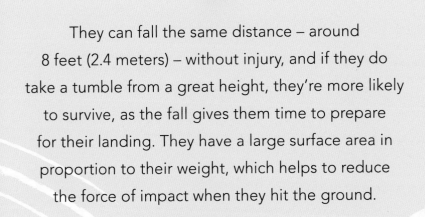

They can fall the same distance – around 8 feet (2.4 meters) – without injury, and if they do take a tumble from a great height, they're more likely to survive, as the fall gives them time to prepare for their landing. They have a large surface area in proportion to their weight, which helps to reduce the force of impact when they hit the ground.

Every cat's nose is unique

Like the human fingerprint, a cat's nose
is made up of bumps and tiny ridges that
can be seen when looked at through a
magnifying glass. No two kitties have the
same noseprint, so if you want to know who
. hogged the cream, check out your cat's nose.

A cat's purr is really a rattle

A cat's purr is the noise of its vocal cords rattling together. Most kitty sounds are made by air pushing past these cords, but the purr is different. This deep rattling mechanism means your cat can breathe easy while purring to its heart's content.

Cats are scared of cucumbers...

And not huge fans of the humble banana either. The smell of the chemicals within the skin of a banana are toxic to a cat. And due to their long and sometimes curved appearance they can also look almost snakelike to the feline eye.

Cats are all heart

Your kitty's heart beats twice as fast as your own. It might be tiny at half the size of a golf ball, but even when it's in super chill mode, it's beating at a pace. The normal heart rate for a healthy pussycat is between 140 and 220 beats per minute.

Cats lick their fur to control their temperature

When it's warm and sunny, a quick lick cools them down, and in the cold it seals in the heat by sticking clumps of fur together. This forms an insulated layer that keeps them toasty from tip to tail.

Cats are in league with the fairies

Cats' eyes were once believed to be portals into the fairy world. If you gazed into them long enough, you might catch a glimpse of the Fairy King or Queen staring back at you. Although it should be said, trying to outstare your cat is not a good idea, unless you want a paw in the face!

Cats are chattier than you think

With a hundred different vocal sounds at their paw-tips, cats are all about the chat. Some moggies mimic their owners, while others imitate the sound of a baby crying, just to get some attention.

Cats are tigers at heart

The domestic moggy shares 95.6 percent of its DNA with the tiger, which explains your kitty's wild side. From body shape and structure to specific patterns on the coat and the way your cat marks its territory, the similarities between your furry friend and this fearsome predator stack up!

Cats can be allergic to humans

People can be allergic to cats, but the reverse is also true. Along with the dead skin cells you shed throughout the day, the chemicals in soap, deodorant, and perfume get right up your cat's nostrils. So if you want to stay sofa snuggle buddies, ditch the smellies and go au naturel.

Cats meow to get our attention

From saying hello to shouting, "Feed me!,"
the power of meow is something every owner
understands. While cats do talk to other cats,
this secret kitty code was created just for
us. It helps your cat state its aim and make
its claim. Whether your moggy is happy,
hungry, or miffed, it's all in the meow.

Cats are tuna addicts

The strong taste and smell make it hard to resist, and cats become hooked to the point that they refuse other foods. It's nice as an occasional treat, but in the long term, it lacks key nutrients and can cause mercury poisoning. Step away from the tin opener now…

Cats smile more than you think

The "slow blink" is where it's at when you are a cat. This one expression, done when gazing into your eyes, is actually a smile, kitty-style. Want to strengthen human-to-cat bonds? Practice often in the company of your pussycat, and you'll notice they return the favor threefold.

Cats are color-blind

It's easy for cats to pick out natural shades like blue and green, but give them a flash of hot pink or scarlet red, and they're kitty clueless. Purple is another mystery and appears blue instead. This is because of a lack of color-sensitive cells known as cones in each retina.

Tabby cats have made their mark

Some of the earliest cats that walked the earth rocked the tabby look. The gene for the patterned coat dates back to the Ottoman Empire in southwest Asia, and soon spread to Europe and Africa. In the eighteenth century, tabby markings became popular in domesticated cats.

Cats like to knead

You might think you're getting a massage kitty-style when your cat is kneading your lap, but this quirky behavior actually stems from kittenhood. Your cat is reverting back to an early reflex, when pummelling Mom's teats helped her produce milk.

Cats sleep a lot!

Cats know those who snooze *never* lose. There's quality to be had in the five-minute nap. Most cats get around fifteen hours of shut-eye a day, which helps them conserve energy and heal wounds. Kittens need more as they're growing, and by the time your cat reaches nine years old, it will have been awake for only three years!

Cats can see when the lights go out

Forget night-vision goggle; when it's pitch-black, your pussycat can see as clear as day thanks to the light receptor rods in each eye. Felines can also expand their pupils, which helps them see and gives them that cute wide-eyed look.

Cats like drinking toilet water

While it's not the best habit to encourage, the reason your cat takes a swig from the toilet bowl is because the water tastes fresh, thanks to the oxygen from each flush. It's also a cooler temperature than water that's been sitting in a food bowl all day.

Your cat's purr is the purrfect medicine

It's all down to the frequency of sound.
The sweet spot is somewhere between 25
and 150 hertz. When your cat's purr falls
into this range, it can help heal broken
bones by improving their density while also
lowering the heart rate, and the good news
is it works for cats and humans alike.

Your cat makes you happier and healthier

Cat owners have lower blood pressure, thanks to the power of the purr. They are also less likely to feel stressed as stroking releases the cuddle hormone oxytocin. This helps to balance emotions and generate those warm fuzzy feelings. Feeling lonely? Cozy up to a cat and you'll easily banish the blues.

Your cat's whiskers really are the cat's whiskers

A face full of whiskers is a plus when you are feline. These wiry hairs are connected to both muscles and the nervous system, and act like a hotline to the brain, sending messages to help your cat navigate the environment. What's more, they're symmetrical, with twelve on each side of the muzzle, so they look pretty too.

Not all cats like catnip

One whiff can send your cat into a frenzy as catnip targets feline "happy receptors" in the brain—but it doesn't work for everyone. It's a hereditary response, but about a third of all kitties don't have the catnip gene. Interestingly, those who do like catnip might also go wacky for olives as they contain a similar chemical compound.

Cats can make your dreams come true

According to the original Italian version
of the Cinderella story, the kindhearted
fairy godmother who helped Cinders go
to the ball was actually a cat! Proof, if any
was needed, that cats are truly magical.

Cats were once witches in disguise

Grimalkin is an archaic term to describe an elderly female pussycat; it was used as an insult for felines with an evil grimace. Derived from the word *malkin*, which refers to a wicked woman, it hints at the link between cats and witches, who were once thought to be one and the same!

Cats always go bottom first

Usually agile and graceful, the tree-climbing moggy must maintain its grip by shuffling down the trunk bottom first. This clumsy descent is thanks to the shape of their claws, which curve downwards, making it impossible for the cat to cling on upside down.

Cats use their whiskers to show you how they feel

Along with detecting changes in the air and helping them feel their way in the dark, whiskers are the go-to barometer for your kitty's mood. A relaxed, happy cat lets it all hang out with downward-drooping whiskers, while a pumped-up pussycat on the prowl will always point them forward.

Cats could survive in the desert

Their ancestral roots mean they've always got the upper paw when it comes to survival skills. Originally desert dwellers, felines are built to endure high temperatures. To conserve water they transpose through their paws and can live on uncooked meat (should the supermarket run out of their favorite brand).

Cats use their butts to say, "Hello"

A bottom in the face might not be our idea of fun, but when your cat presents their booty, it's the feline version of a handshake. Cats have scent glands in that area, and they sniff bottoms as a way of getting to know each other.

Cats and milk do not mix

It might be your cat's favorite tipple, along with a saucer of cream, but it's an upset tummy waiting to happen. Kittens can take it thanks to a gut enzyme that helps them digest the goodness, but adult cats are lactose intolerant and should stick to water.

Cats can have lots of toes

The average cat has five toes on each front paw and four on the back. Some lucky moggies are blessed with up to eight toes on each, which might sound a lot, but for the cat who likes to scratch, catch, and play, it's decidedly pawsome.

Cats know when a storm is coming

This power of perception is rooted in super sensitive hearing and a keen sense of smell, *not* a crystal ball! Cats can detect the scent of rain, while also picking up on subtle atmospheric changes. Thunderclaps can be heard from a great distance, along with the whiff of ozone gas, which often accompanies lightning.

Cats are self-domesticated

As more people worked the land and grain stores increased, so did pests like mice and rats. Never ones to miss an opportunity, cats became the farmer's friend, keeping vermin under control and finding a place in our homes and hearts, while simultaneously feeding their bellies!

Cats know a bit of flab is fab

Your cat's chubby tummy could be good for its health. Excess weight puts a strain on the heart and lungs, but a bit of blubber gives your kitty the edge when it comes to a scrap. All the essential organs are protected, more space is left for food storage, and should your feline take flight instead of fight, the pouch extends to allow extra pounce.

Cats are rubbish at gifting

A dead rodent might not be your idea of a top gift, but it's the purrfect present from your pussycat. In the wild, cat moms look after their young by teaching them how to hunt. As you're part of the family, it's up to your cat to show you how to survive and catch your dinner. Yum…

Cats were once treated like gods

The Egyptians were the crazy cat lovers of the ancient world. Not only did they worship the cat-headed goddess Bast, but when a much-loved moggy died, the entire family would shave off their eyebrows as a mark of respect. Kitties were often mummified and buried with embalmed mice to keep them company in the afterlife.

Cats are nail-biters too

An occasional nail nibble is fine and probably just a mini manicure, but a cat who is always chomping at their claws might have other reasons. Like humans, kitties suffer anxiety, and this, along with boredom, can cause a spell of nail-biting. Lots of reassurance and play are the solution.

Cats think humans are hairless cats

Cats approach us as they would other cats by rubbing against us. They can't distinguish between the different species, but the good news is they don't consider us inferior. They show their respect by nuzzling and brushing up against you, and should a cat roll over and expose their tummy, it's a sign of trust.

Cats use their tails to say, "I love you"

The position of the tail is a giveaway when it comes to feline feelings. A super-chill kitty sticks their tail in the air. Should it quiver at the tip in the same position, then it's "I love you" all the way, but if the tail is thrashing wildly, you've one mad cat on your hands. When it puffs up to twice the size, the fur's about to fly!

About the author

Alison Davies is an author, professional storyteller, and freelance writer from Nottingham, UK. She has penned over forty titles, mostly about animals. Alison also writes for a wide selection of magazines and newspapers about folklore, mythology, and pets. Her features have appeared in *Take a Break Pets* magazine, the *Times Educational Supplement*, and the *Sunday Express*, among others. Her most important and enjoyable role is being cat mom and human of choice to her three furry felines, Ziggy, Diego, and Honey.

About the illustrator

Namasri Niumim is a Thai illustrator based in New Zealand. She graduated with a degree in fine arts and communication design and loves to explore the world, being inspired by the places, plants, and creatures she encounters. Namasri has enjoyed capturing the quirks and personalities of cats using gouache paints.